A souvenir guide

Hidcote

Gloucestershire

National Trust

A Major Garden

Hidcote is one of the country's most celebrated gardens and is known world-wide. While the garden has been well documented, little has been written about its creator, the American anglophile Lawrence Johnston, diligent soldier, passionate gardener and intrepid plant hunter.

Covering an area of 10½ acres (4 hectares), the garden follows Arts and Crafts principles, comprising formal garden 'rooms' around the main house, graduating to a more naturalistic style towards the outer reaches. More unusual is the abundant array of rare and beautiful plants that fill the borders, arranged in a way that was new and exciting for the time, displaying great plantsmanship and artistry.

For many years the only things known about the garden's creator were in a few articles and books that had appeared by the 1980s. Recently, however, research has thrown up more information about Major Lawrence Waterbury Johnston (1871–1958) and why he came to settle in Gloucestershire and create one of the National Trust's most-visited and significant gardens.

A gregarious gardener

Johnston clearly enjoyed the company of his friends, to whom he was devoted. He had an active social life, hosting garden parties around games of tennis, badminton and squash. His considerable artistic abilities were demonstrated in his garden. Tellingly, he is also said to have been well liked by his staff.

Johnston was ultimately a plantsman who forged friendships with other like-minded gardeners. These included but were not limited to: Mark Fenwick of nearby Abbotswood,

Stow-on-the-Wold; Heather Muir from neighbouring Kiftsgate Court; Sir George Holford, founder of Westonbirt Arboretum; Reginald Cory, creator of the notable garden at Dyffryn in South Wales; and the Messels, the great plant-collecting family from Nymans in West Sussex. Johnston was a keen plant hunter, who collected rare and exotic species to furnish his garden. His expeditions led to several introductions not only for Hidcote but also the royal botanic gardens at Edinburgh and Kew.

Esteemed admirers

Accolades from the great and the good are testimony to the success of Johnston's creation. Harold Nicholson and Vita Sackville-West, of Sissinghurst Castle in Kent, were admirers, and Johnston's friend the American novelist Edith Wharton described the garden as 'tormentingly perfect'. In the 1930s the illustrious garden designer Russell Page acknowledged that Hidcote had influenced him more than any other garden, and that Johnston had pushed himself beyond the boundaries of manor-house gardening to plant in bold and unexpected ways.

Right Hidcote is a celebrated garden designed along Arts and Crafts principles

Johnston's early life

That a wealthy American came to settle in the Gloucestershire Cotswolds may be initially surprising. However Lawrence Johnston's unsettled early life may give some clue as to why he put down roots, quite literally, in this idyllic corner of England.

When Johnston was 12 years old his mother Gertrude was divorced, something of a scandal in the strait-laced era into which she was born. However it seems to have been kept undercover and for years it was widely believed that she had been widowed. She was continually on the move back and forth between Europe and America, as was the fashion with wealthy Americans at the time, so the family was never in one place for very long. Besides, she seems not to have had a domestic disposition, preferring the excitement of the many society gatherings in which she circulated.

Gertrude Winthrop

Born into the wealthy New York Waterbury family whose money derived from the rope-making industry, Gertrude was married first to Johnston's father Elliott, who came from an equally wealthy Baltimore banking family. He cut quite a dashing figure, having fought for the Confederate forces of the South in the American Civil War and returned to duty shortly after losing his left foot in the battle of Sharpsburg in 1862. His artificial foot caused

him great pain, so he was encouraged to travel to Europe to find a better fitting one.

After their wedding in Westchester, New York in 1870, Gertrude and Elliott lived in France where Lawrence and his two siblings Elliott and Elizabeth were born, and where sadly Elizabeth died of whooping cough. The marriage soon began to disintegrate and by the mid-1880s, after returning to New York, Elliott and Gertrude were divorced. Both parties subsequently remarried, Gertrude in 1887 to the retired Wall Street banker and stockbroker Charles Francis Winthrop – a surprising match as Frank (as he was better known) had long been considered a confirmed bachelor. After their marriage Gertrude immersed herself in New York society while continuing to enjoy visits to Europe. However, this second marriage was evidently not a success either, as revealed by Frank Winthrop's will, drawn up in 1893, in which he left nothing to Gertrude or his stepsons. Instead he bequeathed his entire estate to his sister.

Her sons' education

Although Gertrude was a wealthy woman in her own right, this blow to her sons' inheritance perhaps turned her thoughts to their future. In 1893, with Elliott studying engineering in Berlin, Gertrude enrolled Lawrence at a private crammer in Little Shelford, near Cambridge, to prepare him for university. He successfully qualified to read history at Trinity College, Cambridge, and graduated in 1897. The following year Johnston travelled north to Northumberland to become a farming pupil, revealing an early inclination for the outdoor life. The same year his stepfather died in Paris. Johnston's own father Elliott died just three years later in 1901, leaving his entire estate to his second wife. Once again he and his brother were excluded from any inheritance.

Above **Lawrence Johnston's father in the uniform of the Confederate forces**

Opposite **Lawrence Johnston and his mother, Gertrude**

A growing interest

Lawrence Johnston forged an army career, seeing action both in the Boer War in South Africa and in the First World War. However, in something of a contrast to his military service, Johnston developed an interest for a more peaceful pastime.

In 1900 Johnston applied to become a British citizen in order to join the Northumberland Hussars, serving as a private in the Boer War. His medical record confirmed that at the age of 28 he was just under 5ft 8in tall and weighed 9st 6lb. Like his father, he proved to be a diligent soldier and was soon promoted to Second Lieutenant. Johnston returned to England and in 1902 settled once again at Little Shelford, lodging with Mr Arthur Gall at Woodville Lodge, where he created a 'beautiful little rock garden' – evidence of his burgeoning interest in gardening.

In 1904 he was elected as a fellow of the Royal Horticultural Society (RHS), frequently borrowing books from the society's library. Initially drawn to alpine plants, he later expanded his interest into plant breeding and gardening in general. Significantly, one of the books he borrowed on more than one occasion was *The Art & Craft of Garden Making* by Thomas H. Mawson, first published in 1900 with new editions appearing until 1926. Other books included *Home and Garden* and *Wood and Garden*, both by the influential garden designer Gertrude Jekyll.

Dutiful son and soldier

Until he reached the retirement age of 50 in 1921, Johnston continued to serve with the Northumberland Hussars, a territorial force with annual two-week summer camps in the years other than those of the Boer War and the First World War. He also visited his mother, who continued to divide her time between Europe and the United States with a lady companion, initially her god-daughter, Ethel Boulton, and later Miss Hedwig von Lekow, the daughter of Baroness von Lekow.

Above Lawrence Johnston after he retired from the Services and was fully able to pursue his real passion

Opposite An early photograph of the Fuchsia Garden, taken in 1910

Arrival at Hidcote

While Johnston was still serving with the Northumberland Hussars, he decided that he needed a more permanent residence. An English manor house and its surrounding estate became the setting for his creation of an outstanding garden.

Johnston and his mother decided to settle in England, opting for the North Cotswolds, where he already had friends, including Mark Fenwick at Abbotswood. The close proximity to the artistic community of fellow American anglophiles who had settled on the village of Broadway in the late 19th century would also have appealed, particularly to the sociable Gertrude. In 1907 a suitable property came up for auction, described in *The Times* advert as a 'very substantial and picturesque farm house,

Above The 1907 sale bill

Above right *A Study of Flowers*, by Lawrence Johnston

stone built, with entrance hall, fine oak staircase, three sitting rooms, eight bedrooms, and usual offices, with lawns and large kitchen garden'. The sales particulars added that the garden contained 'fine shrubs and a nice Summer House, and a large and productive kitchen garden. Adjoining is a Tennis Lawn and small nut orchard.'

Johnston adapted the house to suit their requirements, reconfiguring the layout and adding an extension. Finally he was able to put down roots and practise much of what he had learnt from the many gardening books he had been studying, Thomas H. Mawson's *The Art & Craft of Garden Making* in particular. As there was little existing garden, Johnston effectively had a blank canvas to work with, although he did retain the magnificent cedar tree, which continues to preside over part of the garden to this day.

The development of the garden

Johnston did not draw up an overall plan, preferring to work in phases, first creating intimate garden rooms around the house in the Arts and Crafts style. This area was completed before the outbreak of the First World War, which suspended progress.

Johnston was by now a Major in the Northumberland Hussars and on 5 October 1914 he crossed the Channel with his regiment. Before the month was out, however, he was shot through the right lung at Ypres and came back to London to recover from his wounds. During his recuperation he consumed numerous horticultural volumes borrowed from the conveniently nearby RHS library. He returned to Hidcote for a year before resuming combat in France in 1916, and after his discharge in April 1919 returned to Hidcote, where his mother bought additional farmland, thus enabling Johnston to extend the garden to its present boundary.

Hidcote's heyday

The 1920s and '30s were Hidcote's glory days. The garden layout was completed and Johnston could concentrate on furnishing it with newly discovered plants and exotic rarities, many of which he collected himself on plant-hunting expeditions (see pages 12–13). In 1922 Johnston appointed Frank Adams as head gardener, together with a team of staff, to ensure that the gardens could be maintained to the highest standard. The great and the good

flocked to visit, including the American writer Edith Wharton, the decorator and society hostess Sibyl Colefax, garden designer Norah Lindsay and Vita Sackville-West and Harold Nicholson, who were in the process of creating their own garden at Sissinghurst. Johnston also opened the garden to the public two or three times a year to raise money for various charities, a forerunner of the National Gardens Scheme.

Praised in the press

By 1930 the garden had truly come of age with the publication of two articles in *Country Life* written by Avray Tipping, one of the leading country-house and garden authorities of the day. He expressed his approval of the garden, asserting, 'the gardens are exceptional. They were excellently laid out some 20 years ago, and are admirably maintained.' Four years later an article appeared in *The Listener*, this time by Russell Page, one of the most important garden designers of the 20th century.

Above Lawrence Johnston (on right) *c.* 1927 in Mrs Winthrop's Garden with head gardener Frank Adams

Left and below Two of the illustrations that accompanied a 1930 *Country Life* article

Serre de la Madone

During the early 1920s, Johnston's aged mother Gertrude had taken to spending the winter months in the south of France. With the garden at Hidcote nearing completion it wasn't long before Johnston set himself another challenge with the purchase of land and a villa at Serre de la Madone, near the Mediterranean town of Menton. The steeply terraced garden was a contrast to the flat terrain of his English garden and the warm climate enabled him to grow an even wider range of plants. The land at Serre de la Madone was originally planted with lemon trees, olive groves and vines. His scheme incorporated a shady garden with a long pergola, a Mexican garden, a winter garden with a pool and a formal parterre with four plane trees. Gertrude died at Menton in 1926, just before her 81st birthday, leaving Johnston Hidcote Manor, her money in England and the income from her $2-million estate in the USA, ensuring Johnston's financial security. Her body was brought back to England to be buried in Mickleton churchyard, a mile from Hidcote.

Horticultural influences

Johnston's horticultural bible was Thomas H. Mawson's *The Art & Craft of Garden Making.* **Mawson was a major exponent of the Arts and Crafts style and Johnston followed many of the guidelines advocated in his book.**

In that book Mawson wrote: 'the arrangement should suggest a series of apartments rather than a panorama which can be grasped in one view: art is well directed in arousing curiosity, always inviting further exploration, to be rewarded with new but never a final discovery'. Mawson also recommended formality near the house, gradually softening to merge into the natural landscape beyond by degrees, 'so as to attach the house by imperceptible gradations to the general landscape'.

The two gazebos at the end of the Red Borders at Hidcote reflect Mawson's advice to 'break up a somewhat flat expanse of garden and provide the antidote to a preponderance of horizontal lines, and at the same time supply convenient rest houses … the garden houses are placed equidistant from, and on either side of, the main axial line through the … grounds'.

Mawson's book is illustrated with photographs of garden features, many of which bear similarities to those found at Hidcote. In particular the photograph of the fountain pond at Lewiston Manor in Dorset, showing a circular pond viewed through a pair

of topiary pillars topped with birds, bears close resemblance to the composition of Hidcote's Bathing Pool Garden (see page 28) which in the 1910s had a ground-level pool. Other examples include the lion-mask wall fountain in the Courtyard at Hidcote (see page 22) and the stepping stones in a rock garden, demonstrating the fashion for informal rock gardening, which Johnston adopted in the Upper Stream Garden.

Top The fountain pool at Lewiston Manor, Dorset, could well have been an influence on Lawrence Johnston's Bathing Pool Garden

Above left Thomas H. Mawson

Above right Mawson's version of stepping stones in a rock garden

Parsons and the Broadway connection

Topiary birds were a recurring theme in gardens of the period, including that of Court Farm in nearby Broadway, the home of the American actress Mary Anderson de Navarro from 1896, where she created a garden with the help of the artist and garden designer Alfred Parsons. Like Mawson, Parsons' designs bear all the hallmarks of the period. His style of intimate, planted courtyards, topiary peacocks and pleached lime trees all feature in her garden and would later figure at Hidcote. Mary and Johnston were good friends and there would have been an inevitable exchange of ideas, which she hints at in her book *A Few More Memories*.

Hidcote drew on influences from many of the great plantsmen, garden designers and owners of the period, both at home and abroad, notably in Europe.

By the 1920s Johnston had met the American novelist Edith Wharton, an authority on Italian gardens and the author of *Italian Villas and Their Gardens* (1904). Johnston frequently visited her at her French villa Castel Sainte-Claire in Hyères and at Le Pavillon Colombe, her home near Paris.

Norah Lindsay

One of Lawrence's close friends was Norah Lindsay, garden designer to the aristocracy. She stayed with him several times at Hidcote with her daughter Nancy and visited him at Serre de la Madone, his villa in the south of France. Norah's influence at Hidcote may have led to the increasingly luxuriant planting that Johnston adopted in the 1930s. Nancy also formed a friendship with Johnston, fuelled by their mutual interest in plant collecting, and it was to Nancy that Johnston left his French garden after his death in 1958.

Right Norah Lindsay was another influence and frequent visitor to Hidcote

---

A few of Mary's memories

'Another famous garden is Lawrence Johnston's at Hidcote. The greater part of it is divided up into rooms, as it were, by yew hedges, each "room" containing a wonderful colour scheme. There is also a broad grass path, flanked by high yew hedges; the broad path dips at a gentle incline, then rises until it reaches two pillars with a delicately wrought iron gate – a gate which, standing on the skyline, seems as if it opens on the sky. Lawrence Johnston is a generous gardener and has given me many precious plants. My Italian friends regard Hidcote as the most beautiful garden they have seen in England. Its wonderful blending of colour and its somewhat formal, architectural character please them particularly.'

Mary Anderson de Navarro,
A Few More Memories (1936)

Plant collecting

Johnston read widely and drew on various influences but he was more than a follower of fashion. While the design of the garden at Hidcote epitomises the Arts and Crafts style, it is elevated by his high level of horticultural interest and plantsmanship.

An avid collector with a keen interest in botany, Johnston gained his first RHS award of merit in 1911 for his strain of *Primula pulverulenta*. *The Times* recorded that: 'Of the many new Chinese primroses none has spread from garden to garden so rapidly as *pulverulenta*, but hitherto the typical crimson flowers only were known. The Hidcote strain adds the soft pinks from the *Primula japonica*, at the same time retaining the mealy stem and other characteristics of *pulverulenta*.'

During the 1920s Lawrence diverted his attention to plant-hunting expeditions, including trips to the Drakensburg in South Africa and the Yunnan in China, to collect rare species for both Hidcote and his garden at Serre de la Madone. The new introductions greatly added to Hidcote's appeal both aesthetically and botanically.

A gentleman gardener

Plant hunting was an adventurous pastime that appealed to many leisured gentlemen at the time, many of whom aspired to join the Garden Society, essentially a horticultural gentleman's club. Requirements decreed you had to possess a garden and be actively

engaged in the cultivation, increase and exchange of plants, in particular those recently introduced. Johnston was duly elected in 1922, having been nominated by his friend Mark Fenwick, thus providing him with a network of like-minded gentlemen gardeners with whom to exchange not only ideas but also seeds and plants.

In the same year he undertook his first plant-hunting expedition, to the Swiss Alps. Included in the party was the renowned

Top Lawrence Johnston (centre) and George Taylor (also seated) in an expedition camp in South Africa

Above left Lawrence Johnston on the Forrest expedition to Yunnan

Above right Collected seeds drying before being transported to England

plantsman E. A. Bowles, whose garden at Myddleton House outside London was already well known. In 1927 Johnston travelled to South Africa with Reginald Cory, the creator of Dyffryn Gardens, and the plant collector Collingwood 'Cherry' Ingram as companions, collecting many rare plants not only for their own gardens but for the botanical garden at Edinburgh. In 1929 he travelled to Kenya to climb Mount Kilimanjaro and wrote an article, 'Some Flowering Plants of Kilimanjaro', published in the October 1929 issue of *New Flora and Silva*. His evocative description includes mention of a plant that was to become associated with Hidcote, the yellow-flowered hypericum: 'A very fine dwarf Hypericum, with slender foliage and large, deep, orange-yellow flowers with dashes of red, grew amongst the heather, and may be hardy in our gardens.'

Intrepid explorer?

In 1930 Johnston was a principal sponsor, along with F. C. Stern and Lionel de Rothschild, of a plant-hunting expedition to China by the Scottish botanist George Forrest. In the event, Johnston decided that he wished to go on the expedition to see how it progressed. Johnston, approaching 60 years of age, liked his home comforts and even on expeditions he travelled with his chauffeur and valet. Forrest, a professional plant hunter, complained that Johnston did not pull his weight as he was 'too busy gadding around with Mrs Clerk and others all & every day, riding in the morning, tea and tennis in the afternoon & bridge at the club in the evening'. While this expedition resulted in many new plant introductions including *Mahonia siamensis*, *M. lomariifolia* (see page 45) and *Jasminum polyanthum*, Johnston fell ill with a kidney disease and, much to Forrest's relief, had to return home. Worse was to befall Forrest, who died of a massive heart attack in 1932 while hunting game. Undeterred, Johnston organised and sponsored an expedition to Formosa (modern-day Taiwan) later that year, and the following year was a co-sponsor of an expedition to the Appalachian Mountains in the USA.

Below left *Primula pulverulenta* gained Lawrence his first recognition by the Royal Horticultural Society

Below middle and right *Mahonia siamensis* and *Jasminum polyanthum* were introduced as a result of a 1930 expedition

Entrusted for safe-keeping

By the outbreak of the Second World War Johnston, now in his 70s, was considering moving to France to avoid heavy taxes in the UK. He therefore put his mind to the long-term future of his beloved garden.

Johnston approached James Lees-Milne, the National Trust's Secretary to the Historic Buildings Committee, over lunch in February 1943. Lees-Milne recalls in his diary: '... after lunch, which was delicious, Laurie Johnston took me aside to ask if the National Trust would take over Hidcote garden without an endowment after the war, when he intended to live in the South of France for good. He is a dull little man, and just as I remember him as a child. Mother-ridden. Mrs Winthrop, swathed in grey satin from neck to ankle, would never let him out of her sight.'

Despite these less than kind words, a few months later Lees-Milne acknowledges the outstanding contribution this 'dull little man' made to British gardens. Following his visit of Tuesday 6 July 1943, he recorded: 'Papa drove me to Hidcote to tea with Laurie Johnston who took us round his famous garden. No reference was made by him to the National Trust. The garden is not only beautiful but remarkable in that it is full of surprises. You are constantly led from one scene to another, into long vistas and little enclosures, which seem infinite. Moreover the total area of this garden does not cover many acres. Surely the 20th century has produced some

remarkable gardens on a small scale. This one is also full of rare plants brought from the most outlandish places in India and Asia. When my father and Laurie Johnston were absorbed in talk I was tremendously impressed by their profound knowledge of a subject which is closed to me. It was like hearing two people speaking fluently a language of which I am totally ignorant.'

Nothing happened in 1943, but in 1947 Lees-Milne was again approached to handle the sensitive negotiations.

Above James Lees-Milne oversaw negotiations that saw Hidcote transferred to the National Trust

A memorial to the Major

The National Trust was initially reluctant to
take on a garden without an endowment.
In 1948 however, after much deliberation,
it acquired Hidcote as the first garden of
national importance to be taken on under a
Gardens Fund, launched jointly by the Trust
and the Royal Horticultural Society to save
such gardens. This initiative was publically
announced at the Annual General Meeting
of the RHS on 17 February 1948. It was on this
same occasion that Lord Aberconway, the
President of the RHS, presented the Veitch
Gold Medal to Johnston, pronouncing that:
'There has been no more beautiful formal
garden laid out since the time of the old
Palace of Versailles than that designed on
quite a small scale, but with exquisite artistry,
by Major Lawrence Johnston at Hidcote.'

Johnston died at Serre de la Madone 10
years later in 1958 and is buried alongside his
mother at Mickleton.

Above Lawrence
Johnston's gift to the
nation represents one
of the most important
gardens in the country

Left A 1951 edition of *The
National Trust* magazine
sporting Hidcote on its
front cover

Restoring the garden

Hidcote has now been under the
custodianship of the National Trust for a
longer period than Lawrence Johnston's
ownership, and naturally during this time
attitudes towards conservation have evolved.
The garden had suffered from a gradual
decline since the 1940s, with the death of
Frank Adams the head gardener in 1939 and
Johnston moving to Serre in 1948. In 1956 the
great plantsman and Gardens Adviser for the
National Trust Graham Stuart Thomas (see
also page 17) was given the responsibility of
overseeing the garden. He ensured that a high
level of horticultural skill was employed and
the planting was to the highest standard of the
day. Recently however, the policy has been to
return the gardens to as close a representation
as possible of Johnston's creation in its heyday
of the 1930s, with the restoration of several
buildings and garden areas. One of the most
significant features to be restored is the Plant
House (see page 42), which was damaged in a
storm and removed in the 1950s, but which
highlighted Johnston's love of rare and exotic
plants. The Tennis Court has also been
reinstated, recalling the house and garden
parties enjoyed by Johnston and his friends.

Johnston's legacy

At first sight Hidcote appears to be the archetypal Arts and Crafts garden of the sort that flourished in and around the Cotswolds during the Victorian and Edwardian eras. However, a closer look reveals a garden that stands out from the others.

Johnston had a serious interest in plants and plant collecting, and he introduced over 70 plants into cultivation. Several of these, such as *Hypericum* 'Hidcote', *Lavendula* 'Hidcote' and *Verbena* 'Lawrence Johnston' have remained staples in British gardens to this day.

Below left
Hypericum 'Hidcote'

Below middle
Lavendula 'Hidcote'

Below right *Verbena* 'Lawrence Johnston'

Gardening on a higher plane

'Here he planted the higher parts of the ground with large groups of many kinds of berberis … but what lifted this scheme onto a higher plane were tufts and groups of Yuccas…. Exotically Mexican, their sharp foliage and creamy candelabra spikes of flowers defied the expected and made a new kind of world, apt for setting a flock of rosy pink flamingos unbelievably wading in the shallow pond which was the centre of this garden.'

Russell Page describing the Wilderness, *The Education of a Gardener* (1962)

Horticultural history

The most important principles that Johnston gardened by were to 'plant only the best forms of any plant', to 'plant thickly' in the knowledge that bare earth would encourage weeds, and to 'compose plantings from all types of plants'.

Graham Stuart Thomas, Gardens Adviser for the National Trust, described the strong design of the garden on a visit during its 1930s heyday: 'There would be one plant climbing over another, a group of disparate shrubs united by a continuous under-planting of some lowly flower; there would seldom be a single clump of any herbaceous plant or bulb, rather it would be grouped here and there creating the effect of having sown itself; the colours were and are mostly blended into separate schemes with occasionally a deliberate clash. Seldom is one plant given one whole piece of ground; it shares it with others. All this hangs together because of the firm design, which is so much enhanced by the vertical lines of dark evergreen hollies and holm oaks.'

It was this combination of strong form together with luxuriant planting that was to prevail throughout the 20th century, and it was at Hidcote that the Trust first developed its approach to the conservation of important historic flower gardens.

Right Graham Stuart Thomas, Gardens Adviser for the National Trust in the 1950s

A garden with house attached

Before we get into the garden and its complex of rooms and wildernesses and vistas and wide-open spaces, it's worth taking a moment to consider Johnston's modifications to the manor house at Hidcote.

The manor house was originally a late 17th-century farmhouse remodelled with a formal façade in the late 18th and early 19th centuries. When Johnston and his mother bought the manor the entrance was via the main façade facing the village road. During the first few years after their arrival, an extension was constructed, almost doubling the size. The steps leading

from the village road were removed, the gateway blocked and the height of the wall raised, leaving the section immediately in front of the door lowered to retain the view of the lime avenue with the statue of Hercules beyond. Behind the wall he created the East Court Garden, a small cobbled parterre garden (see page 22). The main entrance was re-sited to the side of the old wing, now approached from the Courtyard, using a salvaged 18th-century door. Above this he placed a coat of arms inscribed with his motto *semper paratus ad arma* ('always prepared for arms'), the same coat of arms and motto that Johnston's aunt Harriet Lane Johnston used on her correspondence. (Harriet Lane before her marriage had been First Lady to US President James Buchanan.)

Making an entrance

The original flag-stoned Courtyard was re-invented by Johnston as a more inviting gravel entrance court, softening the outbuildings with swags of climbing plants and ornamenting the far wall with a lion-mask fountain (see page 22).

A building on the east wall of the Courtyard was originally a stable or barn, but was made into a plant house by replacing the Courtyard side of the roof with glass, described in the 1930s as 'a low but ample shed converted into a camellia house, with space left in it to accommodate a luncheon table (Avray Tipping, *Country Life*, 1930). The building was demolished in 1943 and today there is a plant border in its place.

The 18th-century stone and brick barn with granary above in the south-east corner was converted by Johnston into a chapel (Johnston having by that time converted to Catholicism). The National Trust shop (at the southern end of the western range of buildings) was one of the original barns. Johnston converted another of the barns into a squash court and another into a badminton court.

Tour of the Garden

Hidcote is a revelatory experience, taking the visitor on a journey from intimate formal areas around the house to the naturalistic wider spaces further afield. Johnston's plant-hunting expeditions are echoed in exotic planting, but occasional views of the pastoral landscape beyond ensure that the sense of place is never lost.

The Rock Bank and the view across the surrounding parkland

Early enclosures

The manor house sits between two enclosed courtyards, preparing you for some of the intimacy and enclosed formality of the Arts and Crafts-style garden rooms close to the house.

The Courtyard

The Courtyard is the first impression of the garden, informally laid out and enclosed by the house and barns. Over the gate-piers scrambles the rambling rose 'François Juranville', with its copper-tinted leaves and coral-pink flowers. *Magnolia delavayi* (see page 44), one of Johnston's original plantings, is grown together with *Mahonia lomariifolia*. A grey-leaved red-hot poker *Kniphofia caulescens* grows in the bed against the boundary wall. The evergreen climber *Schizophragma hydrangeoides* var. *hydrangeoides* 'Roseum' flowers against the chapel wall adorned in spring with the

bluebell-like flowers of *Clematis alpina*. In April the south wall is adorned with *Viburnum* x *burkwoodii* in full flower, to be followed by a fine display from the wisteria trained over the shop exit and the old climbing rose 'Gloire de Dijon'.

The East Court Garden

Entering the garden through the house you come to the East Court Garden, probably one of the first areas to be laid out. It was reinstated in 2006–7. Tipping in his 1930 *Country Life* article describes a 'flowering Parterre' with 'box-edged squares … bedded with lavender-blue nemesias and *Petunia* 'Silver Lilac', from which rise standards of heliotrope … with great tubs of pink *Hydrangea hortensis* at the corners'. However, by 1934 Russell Page noted a different scene: 'a huge variegated silver holly overshadows this narrow strip of ground and provides the theme for a tiny formal garden. Four beds edged with the low-growing variegated euonymus, are divided by cobbled paths … planted out in spring with silvery mauve violas', followed by 'pink begonias and … montbretias'.

Today the planting includes the Californian poppy *Carpenteria californica*, *Deutzia* x *hybrida* 'Mont Rose' and *Sorbaria sorbifolia*.

Left The view into the Courtyard in 1930

Below *Carpenteria californica*

Above *Sorbaria sorbifolia*

Left The lion-mask fountain of local materials in the Courtyard is a further nod to the Arts and Crafts principles along which the garden is designed

Opposite The view from the East Court Garden along the lime avenue to the statue of Hercules

By the old manor

These areas close to the house display traditional manor-house gardening, with generous swathes of successional planting softening the edges but still with each area having its own distinct feel and theme.

The Old Garden

The border under the house wall awakens in spring with mixed narcissus and *Lathyrus vernus*, followed by blue camassias and white oriental poppies. Early in the summer the climbing *Rosa* 'Lawrence Johnston' (see page 45), raised in France in 1923, furnishes the wall, bearing large semi-double flowers of bright clear yellow.

In the narrow border close to the cottages on the far side, Johnston planted acid-loving species, including exotic blue Himalayan poppies (*Meconopsis* spp.), having first created special soil to suit the plants.

A fine *Magnolia sieboldii* subsp. *sinensis* is underplanted with hellebores and *Anemone blanda*, while erythroniums, cyclamen and *Bergenia ciliata* flourish in the shade of the wall. The two borders at the centre are being rejuvenated to Johnston's original scheme, enhanced by tulip varieties from the 1930s and 1940s.

The Maple Garden

Dwarf Japanese maples (*Acer palmatum* var. *dissectum*) give their name to the garden, their delicate foliage complemented by the white-flowered *Magnolia stellata* and a variety of rhododendrons. Two rectangular beds are filled with blue hyacinths in the spring, replaced in the summer with the vanilla-scented *Heliotropium* 'Lord Robert'.

To the south, close to the wall, a gravel path leads past a sunken stream where the bold yellow-flowered skunk cabbage and elegant Solomon's seal flourish.

A fine *Staphylea holocarpa* var. *rosea* is on the right as you leave the garden, introduced into cultivation from China in 1908. In June the yew tree by the stream is furnished with a confetti-like profusion of pale-pink flowers from the rambling *Rosa* 'Paul's Himalayan Musk'.

The White Garden

The magnificent old cedar tree dominates this small and intricate garden guarded by four now dumpy topiary birds. Under the cedar is a tapestry of *Dicentra spectabilis*, scillas, *Anemone blanda* and violets.

This garden, established by 1910, was originally referred to as the phlox garden and photographs taken in 1915 show it planted with blue, purple and white phlox, edged with pale blue pansies. It is uncertain when this became the White Garden. It seems the phlox were removed due to an infestation of eelworm, but in time the phlox will be reinstated.

Left The White Garden

Right The entrance to the Old Garden as shown in *Country Life* in 1930

The central axis

Right Looking through the south gazebo down the Long Walk

Opposite The Red Borders aflame with colour in June

Here Lawrence Johnston's ambitions for his garden at Hidcote start to open up and reveal themselves, treating the visitor to long, framed views and to exciting shapes and contrasting colours structured in eye-catching ways.

The Lilac Circle

The Lilac Circle is a pivotal point where a secondary axis converges with the central axis. A circular lawn edged with a brick path is bordered by beds of flag iris, backed by a row of Rouen lilacs (*Syringa* x *chinensis*), a showstopper in May. In the summer the powder-blue flowers of the deciduous *Ceanothus* x *delileanus* 'Gloire de Versailles' and an edging of *Lavandula angustifolia* 'Munstead' are enlivened with spangles of orange and yellow Welsh poppies. The whole area is enclosed within a holly and copper beech hedge.

The Red Borders

To the west of the Lilac Circle a path leads you to the twin Red Borders, created between 1910 and 1914 and originally designed as 'scarlet borders'. In his 1934 article, Russell Page noted the borders were planted 'almost entirely in reds and oranges for late summer colour'.

Today the planting reaches its peak in mid-summer, when tender exotics such as cordylines, cannas and lobelias are reinstated after wintering under glass. The borders are a blend of the whole spectrum of reds, from the fiery orange-red *Hemerocallis fulva* 'Flore Pleno'

Hemerocallis fulva 'Flore Pleno'

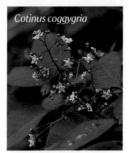
Cotinus coggygria

Rosa 'Evelyn Fison'

Papaver orientale '(Goliath Group) Beauty of Livermere'

to the deep wine-red of *Clematis* 'Kermesina'. Highlights of bright scarlet from *Lychnis chalcedonica* and the *Rosa* 'Evelyn Fison' are tempered with an occasional green foil from evergreens, such as the dwarf mountain pine *Pinus mugo* and the stately *Yucca gloriosa*.

In these borders foliage is as important as flowers and the red theme is carried through to the purple-leaved smoke bush *Cotinus coggygria* and the giant rhubarb *Rheum palmatum* 'Atrosanguineum', whose mature green leaves are flushed with red on the undersides. The stately *Dahlia* 'Bishop of Llandaff' has the advantage of both, with bright crimson flowers emerging from foliage of darkest purple, providing interest from late summer until the first frost. In the original scheme, other late flowers included the scarlet *Verbena* 'Lawrence Johnston', which matched the red of the rosehips in autumn, while in spring the borders are brought to life by flowering cherries, a fine display of red and purple tulips and the magnificent oriental poppy, *Papaver orientale* '(Goliath Group) Beauty of Livermere'.

The Gazebos

The lawn between the Red Borders leads up to a pair of red-brick gazebos, created by Johnston in 1914. Such structures recall features found in 16th- and 17th-century gardens. The north gazebo is tiled with antique Delft tiles and panels, one depicting a vase of flowers and the other a ship. The south gazebo is in effect a portico through which you can access the Long Walk to the south; inside the gazebo is a plaque recording Johnston's gift of Hidcote to the Trust.

The Stilt Garden

Beyond the gazebos the main axis becomes a lawn flanked by pleached hornbeams. The little borders around the pavilions are planted with *Helleborus corsicus* and in the beds at the western end are the yellow crown imperial fritillary, 'Maxima Lutea', together with the lofty grasses *Miscanthus sinensis* and *Stipa gigantea*. An elegant wrought-iron gate known as Heaven's Gate affords views out over the parkland towards the Malvern Hills.

Private spaces

The sense of intimacy grows even deeper as the visitor steps through the walls of yew that enclose these garden rooms. Within these spaces it is easy to feel that one is within a quite different garden as their characters are so distinct and individual.

The Fuchsia Garden

Situated between the Lilac Circle and the Pool Garden, the Fuchsia Garden was created in the first phase of garden making, around 1910. It was laid out simply as a formal parterre with four box-edged beds around a central circular bed, enclosed by a tapestry hedge of green and copper beech together with variegated holly and box. The yew topiary birds, which have become a symbol of the garden, flank the steps to the Bathing Pool. Originally planted with annuals, then roses, by the 1940s the garden was replanted with fuchsias. The variegated fuchsia *F. magellanica* var. *gracilis* 'Variegata' features in the centre beds, 'Tom Thumb' is in the triangular beds to the right, with 'Lady Thumb' to the left. To extend the season of interest today, the fuchsias are underplanted with a carpet of blue *Scilla sibirica*.

The Bathing Pool Garden

The Fuchsia Garden leads to the Bathing Pool Garden, also created in the first phase of garden making and dating from before 1910. Originally conceived as a sunken garden set around a small ground-level circular pool with six wedge-shaped beds radiating out on one side, the whole area was simplified in 1921 and the pool was raised to provide a swimming pool with a deeper end for diving, enjoyed by the Muir girls from neighbouring Kiftsgate

Above *Fuchsia* 'Tom Thumb'

Left The Fuchsia Garden, *c*.1930

Below Bathers enjoying the pool

Above The Bathing
Pool Garden

Court. By 1930 the pool was given a fountain in the form of a boy and a dolphin, a direct reference to the photograph in Mawson's *The Art & Craft of Garden Making*.

The planting includes *Magnolia* x *soulangeana*, azaleas, cream hydrangeas and tree peonies. White 'Iceberg' roses flank the steps down to the garden and in the narrow, shady, acid border beyond the pool Johnston successfully planted the blue poppies *Meconopsis grandis* and *M. baileyi*, which had recently been introduced to this country by the plant hunter Frank Kingdon-Ward, to be followed by blue gentians *Gentiana asclepiadea* and the white bugbane *Cimicifuga racemosa*. The unusual white *Corydalis ochroleuca* has gently colonised the walls.

The Italian Shelter
To the side of the Bathing Pool Garden is a thatched stone loggia, known as the Italian Shelter, which was built in the 1910s. It was originally painted with a *tromp l'oeil* mural which has now completely faded. It is set within its own little courtyard and adorned with terracotta pots planted with the giant-leaved *Hosta sieboldii*.

The Poppy Garden
Hostas, including *H. lancifolia* and *H. ventricosa*, and the large *Hydrangea aspera* Villosa Group dominate this space. Blue camassias and the pink-flowering cherry *Prunus* 'Kanzan' add a dash of colour in spring and a large-leaved *Vitis coignetiae* (crimson glory vine) trails through the yew hedge and sets the garden ablaze with colour in the autumn.

The Green Circle
This is the final garden on the secondary axis and is a simple, enclosed circular space with a central lawn. A solitary painted iron seat provides a pause amongst the abundant glories of the garden.

Inspired by the Alpes-Maritimes

These areas display some of Hidcote's more exotic plantings, reminiscent of Johnston's garden in the south of France. They come as something of a surprise – and a challenge – in a Gloucestershire garden.

The Alpine Terrace

Running parallel to the Stilt Garden is a wide gravel walk enclosed within a beech hedge. Here are two tiered raised beds, protected from winter rain by glass covers enabling a range of rare alpines and succulents to be grown, including brightly coloured varieties of *Lewisia*, yellow-flowered drabas and South African *Rhodohypoxis*.

At the end by the gazebo is a magnificent example of the pineapple broom *Argyrocytisus battandieri* (see page 45), its silver foliage further illuminated in June with bright yellow, pineapple-scented flowers.

Below left The Alpine Terrace

Below right A pergola on a terrace at Serre de la Madone

Opposite left The terraces at Serre de la Madone

Opposite right The Rock Bank and Bulb Slope were inspired by Lawrence Johnston's garden in the Alpes-Maritimes

The Rock Bank and Bulb Slope

The recently renovated Rock Bank has been reinstated to reflect Johnston's original design inspired by a Mediterranean hillside, using plants that thrive in hot, dry conditions. Here rock roses flourish, including *Helianthemum* 'Wisley Primrose' and *Cistus* x *hybridus*. Sea hollies, ferns and irises are scattered throughout the rock strata with a clump of the angelica tree *Aralia elata* planted near the top. Below are primulas, the exquisite black-flowered *Iris chrysographes* and a carpet of bright blue navelwort, *Omphalodes cappadocica*. In the autumn the evergreen *Viburnum davidii* is furnished with blue berries, while blue gentians flower in the scree below.

Beyond the Rock Bank is a lawn planted with small trees, including juniper and the smoke bush, *Cotinus coggygria*.

Herbaceous planting at the edge leads to the Bulb Slope lower down. An informal array of bulbs including camassias, *Anemone pavonina* and daffodils, create a riot of colour in the spring. Blue and white campanulas together with martagon lilies extend the season into July. By autumn it is alight with the fiery autumn foliage of Japanese maples, cherries and, at the bottom of the slope, the orange hues of the Indian chestnut tree, *Aesculus indica*.

Southern exposure

Right Mrs Winthrop's Garden is an intimate, enclosed space which affords views into the Wilderness

Below The Pillar Garden with the purple *Allium hollandicum* 'Purple Sensation' in the foreground

These gardens, enclosed and enjoying a southerly aspect, afford the opportunity to grow tender species that might otherwise struggle in the English climate. Their special characters create garden rooms that are both highly unusual and intimate.

The Pillar Garden

Johnston created the Pillar Garden in about 1923. It is named after the regimented rows of tightly clipped yew pillars, which are planted on a series of shallow terraces, the whole enclosed by a beech hedge to the north and a hornbeam hedge to the east. The large *Magnolia denudata* together with *Narcissus* 'Actaea', 'Flower Record' and 'La Riante' ensure that there is plenty of interest in early spring.

The garden is at its peak in May when peonies spill over the paths, followed by fragrant lilies and spheres of purple *Allium hollandicum* hovering above the foliage. The fastigiate (narrowing toward the top) 'Amanogawa' cherries rise through mounds of *Geranium* 'Johnson's Blue' planted at their bases, and by June the heady scent of mock orange *Philadelphus* 'Belle Etoile' and *P.* 'Beauclerk' fills the air. In the autumn fuchsias take over together with pink nerines in the narrow border by the lawn.

Mrs Winthrop's Garden

Johnston designed this garden to be a warm sunny place for his mother to sit. Based on the familiar pattern of a circle within a square, it is enclosed within beech, both green and copper, and lime hedges on three sides and open on the south side. Brick paths lead towards a sundial in the centre. Yellow, Mrs Winthrop's favourite colour, was the original theme. Later blue was incorporated as a contrast. The golden creeping Jenny *Lysimachia nummularia* 'Aurea' scrambles through the low beds, while pillars of golden hop supported on tripods punctuate the corners. Yellow-flowered *Hypericum* 'Hidcote' (see page 16), *Calceolaria integrifolia* and *Allium moly* are offset by blue monkshood *Aconitum napellus*, *Salvia patens* 'Cambridge Blue' and *Allium caeruleum*. A Mediterranean flavour is achieved with the addition of terracotta pots planted with agaves and trachycarpus palms.

Into the wild

The formality of the garden rooms closer to the house falls away here as the areas become more expansive and expressive of a more naturalistic style of planting, the contrast making the garden seem even greater in extent and variety.

The Wilderness

The Wilderness was also known as Westonbirt after the famous arboretum in Gloucestershire, said to be the inspiration for this particular part of the garden. It was one of the last areas of the garden to be made and provided a rather exotic twist, described by Norah Lindsay in 1948 as 'a Himalayan fairyland'.

Originally planted for autumn colour, the garden contains huge colonies of colchicums, a large *Cercidiphyllum japonicum* tree (whose crushed leaves smell of burnt toffee), pampas grass, liquidambers, and the bright red, orange and pink berries of the spindle *Euonymus europaeus*. Today there is plenty of year-round interest. April comes alive with the blossom of the spreading white-flowered cherry *Prunus* 'Shimidsu-zakura' and the vibrant pink foliage of *Acer pseudoplatanus* 'Brilliantissimum'. Later in the summer *Hydrangea aspera* subsp. *sargentiana* puts on a flamboyant display of large, flat-headed mauve flowers. Even in the winter months tree bark of varying colour and texture ensures there is plenty to see, from *Acer griseum* which has cinnamon-coloured bark peeling from the trunk to the snake bark of *Acer grosseri* var. *hersii*, striped green and white.

Originally the home to Johnston's collection of ornamental fowl, which included flamingos, golden pheasant and an ostrich, the Wilderness still attracts birds today but now only those of the wild variety.

Left The Wilderness is especially spectacular with its autumn foliage

The Upper and Lower Stream Gardens

The meandering paths of the Stream Gardens are a contrast to the formal garden rooms nearer the house.

The Upper Stream Garden below Mrs Winthrop's Garden is alive with tall elegant spires of francoas and the chalky white perovskias together with white lacecap hydrangeas.

On the western side of the Long Walk, the Lower Stream Garden is ablaze in spring with blue-flowered brunneras, yellow trilliums and yellow skunk lily, tempered with elegant fronds of unfurling ferns. Primulas and periwinkles shelter under the stately leaves of the bronze *Rodgersia pinnata* 'Superba'. Trees and shrubs contributing to the spring flourish include *Magnolia denudata*, rhododendrons and azaleas. Later in the year the pale yellow, shuttlecock flowers of the elegant *Kirengeshoma palmata* emerge. *Ligularia dentata* 'Desdemona' can be found with its sombre round dark foliage contrasting with its bright orange flowers. By the bridge is the largest Indian horse chestnut tree (*Aesculus indica*) in Britain.

Fern Dell

Replanted in 2008, the Fern Dell is protected by a holly hedge on the eastern side and the Lime Arbour to the west. It was created on the north side of the Upper Stream Garden with banks clothed in violet-coloured hydrangeas, junipers and cedar trees. Ferns thrive in the damp air – including exotic tree ferns – and in winter the banks are carpeted with snowdrops.

Right The Lower Stream Garden

Open spaces

While many areas of the garden delight with detailed, abundant and luxuriant planting, there are others in which the visitor can enjoy the simple pleasure of the great outdoors and long vistas framed by statuesque features, hedges and trees.

The Long Walk

As a contrast to the tapestry of garden rooms and abundant borders, this long tranquil stretch of lawn enclosed within clipped hornbeam hedges rises towards a stately wrought-iron gate and through to the pastoral landscape beyond. Brick pillars topped with pineapple-shaped finials frame the view.

This page The Long Walk

Opposite left The Great Lawn has been put to various uses over the years

The Great Lawn

A further green space is the vast lawn framed by a tightly clipped yew hedge. A semi-circular apse at the western end has been planted with a clump of beech trees, and a flight of stone steps leads up to 'the bandstand'. A small concession to colour within this strict green regime can be found in September when a few autumn crocuses dare to emerge around the beech trees. This space was used by Johnston for bowls. During the Second World War the Great Lawn was dug up and planted with potatoes. Latterly the National Trust has made good use of the theatre-like layout, hosting plays and concerts here.

The Beech Allée

A wrought-iron gate to the north of the Great Lawn leads to the Beech Allée, which in turn leads to a pair of wooden gates, one of several to be found in the garden that were probably copied from nearby Cleeve Prior Manor. Johnston is likely to have seen the gates as they featured in Gertrude Jekyll and Lawrence Weaver's book, *Gardens for Small Country Houses* (1912). In the summer the Beech Allée provides a shady retreat from the sun and is transformed in the autumn with a crisp golden carpet of fallen leaves.

The Lime Arbour

Johnston cleverly manipulated perspective in the Lime Arbour by gradually reducing the width of the path at the southern end – thereby visually, if not literally, increasing its length.

The Beech Allée

Purely productive

While Hidcote is mostly a garden that appeals to gardeners and plantsmen, there are areas that are more edible than ornamental. That said, these are still pleasant places in which to walk and admire nature's bounty.

A prerequisite of the country house was a generous kitchen garden to feed the multitude of guests, whether invited for lunch, for a game of tennis or to stay. The Kitchen Garden at Hidcote was, perhaps surprisingly, large enough to supply four hospitals during the Second World War.

When the Trust took over, the garden was used to propagate plants for exchange. Recently the Kitchen Garden has been restored and today it supplies fruit and vegetables for use in the restaurant. The greenhouse is also used to overwinter tender plants before they are brought out in the summer. The adjoining orchard contains many old varieties of apples, most of which are pressed into juice for sale in the shop.

Johnston's tennis court is also tucked away next to the kitchen garden and has now been restored. Energetic visitors are welcome to use the court.

Opposite Sweet peas in the Kitchen Garden in July

Right Johnston hosted many tennis parties and today's visitors are welcome to have a game

Below The orchard

Delightfully decorative

After the more functional areas of the garden, it's a pleasure to once again find yourself in an area of the garden dedicated to a single purpose. The Long Borders serve only to delight and excite the senses through the interplay of colour and scent.

Created out of an old orchard where a few of the existing old apple trees remain to this day, the Long Borders, or Rose Walk as it was also called, was the last area of the garden to be planted, in the 1930s and 1940s. Johnston transformed the garden, with the help of Norah Lindsay, into a pair of 30-foot wide borders planted with old varieties of French roses. Visiting the garden in 1949 Vita Sackville-West observed that Johnston 'grew these enchanting varieties years before they became the fashion and his collection includes many which are still hard to obtain'.

At the entrance stands a magnificent old false acacia *Robinia* x *ambigua* 'Decaisneana'. Its tassels of pink pea-like flowers are worth looking out for in June. Staggered pillars of Irish yews provide structure and rhythm to the borders. These are interplanted with lilacs, including the single, dark-purple *Syringa vulgaris* 'Andenken an Ludwig Späth' and the pale lilac *Syringa* 'Captain Baltet'.

In spring narcissus, auriculas and grape hyacinths embroider the borders through drifts of purple sage. At the far end of the path dividing the borders a pretty white seat is flanked by two standard wisterias, their white

Syringa vulgaris 'Andenken an Ludwig Späth'

Rosa 'Tuscany Superb'

Rosa 'La Ville de Bruxelles'

Rosa 'William Lobb'

Rosa 'St Nicholas'

racemes cascading overhead in May. Most of the roses flower only for a short period in June but they are well worth the wait. Included in the gallicas are 'Surpasse Tout' which has deepest red petals, paling with age, 'Marcel Bourgouin' and the popular 'Tuscany Superb', both with semi-double, blood-red flowers.

Of the damasks the single, pink 'St Nicholas' was bred by Johnston's friend Bobbie James and has the added bonus of having a second flush of flowers. 'Mme Zoetmans' has double, shell-pink flowers with green eyes and 'La Ville de Bruxelles' is a richer pink with a heady perfume. The curious moss roses are represented by 'William Lobb' with buds seemingly engulfed in moss. 'Lanei' has double, deep-crimson flowers and 'A Longues Pedoncules' has, as its name suggests, long mossy flower stalks and pale pink blooms. The roses are succeeded by *Penstemon* 'Andenken an Friedrich Hahn' of deepest red, the mouth-watering 'Sour Grapes' and 'Hidcote Pink'.

Around the houses

On the approach back to the manor house, the outbuildings and the Garden Yard are more obviously the gardeners' territory, with the nurseries and workshops and stores required to maintain a garden as large and complex as Hidcote.

The Plant House

Situated to the north of the Great Lawn, the Plant House was erected to protect Johnston's collection of tender plants, with vertical glass panels that could be removed throughout the summer months, giving it more the appearance of a pergola. It was an impressive structure and very much part of the ornamental garden. Full of unusual plants and ornamental pots, Johnston could imagine himself back in one of his far-flung expeditions. The Plant House was removed in the 1950s having suffered storm damage but was rebuilt in 2006 in tribute to Johnston's plant-hunting adventures.

It is one of the best recorded areas of the garden and today the Plant House is filled once again with an array of tender plants, including pots of citrus trees, a yellow-flowered Peruvian angel's trumpet (*Brugmansia* sp.), the purple-flowered *Grewia occidentalis*, the pink Chilean bellflowers (*Lapageria rosea)*, the succulent moonstone plant (*Pachyphytum oviferum*) and the elegant vine lilac (*Hardenbergia violacea*).

The Pine Garden and Lily Pool

Bay trees in Versailles planters, agaves in terracotta pots and an abundance of grey-foliaged plants give this area a distinctly Mediterranean flavour. The small circular beds are filled with rock roses, including pink-flowered cistuses and double-yellow helianthemums. In spring the beautiful lemon-yellow peony 'Molly the Witch' (*Paeonia mlokosewitschii*) flowers in the borders around the pool, alongside huge stone troughs full of thrift and succulent sempervivums.

Above The Lily Pool in front of the Plant House

Left The Plant House in 1930

The Garden Yard

This was the service area with timber buildings used as the tool shed and head gardener's office. Johnston's original planting of *Wisteria floribunda* 'Multijuga' spills over the sheds, dripping with blue flowers in May. Against the thatched barn the fine handkerchief tree, *Davidia involucrata* (see next page), also puts on a show in May with a display of huge white bracts. In the borders below, purple liriopes and Japanese anemones ensure plenty of colour through the autumn.

Against the shop wall is an unusual false acacia, *Robinia* x *holdtii*, underplanted with philadelphus and *Lathyrus vernus*. Versailles planters and an old lead water tank dated 1706 are planted up variously with heliotropes, fuschias, hyacinths and tulips for a flamboyant summer display.

How Does Our Garden Grow?

There is something to see all year round at Hidcote, including much of Johnston's original planting. These rare specimens together with familiar garden hybrids represent Johnston's connoisseurship and diversity as a plantsman.

Winter/Spring

Spring

Magnolia campbellii

Magnolia delavayi

Osmanthus yunnanensis

Davidia involucrata

Summer

Wisteria floribunda 'Alba'

Lavendula 'Hidcote Giant'

Summer/Autumn

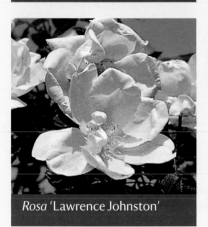

Rosa 'Lawrence Johnston'

Argyrocytisus battandieri

Anemone x *hybrida* 'Honorine Jobert'

Autumn/Winter

Colchium spp.

Mahonia lomariifolia

Berberis thunbergii f. *atropurpurea*

Gardening today

Lawrence Johnston had a large team of gardeners and farm labourers to help develop and maintain his garden. However, when the National Trust took over there were only five gardeners. Maintenance of the garden had to be adapted accordingly, with the paring down of many areas and the planting palette simplified.

Below Mrs Winthrop and her staff

Bottom Lawrence Johnston with his gardeners and dogs

For the gardeners and their helpers

There are 4½ miles of hedging at Hidcote, which takes up to five months to cut with electric hedge-trimmers.

Around 16,000 bulbs are planted every autumn to provide a colourful display in spring and summer.

The gardeners propagate about 85 per cent of their plant requirements every year.

The Kitchen Garden helps to provide the restaurant with fruit and vegetables, while apples from the orchard are pressed to make juice for sale in the shop.

Beehives in the garden aid pollination and provide local honey.

Wildlife is encouraged throughout the garden to encourage natural predators, and nesting boxes are provided to support local bird populations. Here pallets and an assortment of locally gathered materials are arranged to attract insects.

Greener gardening

In line with National Trust policy, Hidcote is run as sustainably as possible to meet the modern-day challenges of increased visitor numbers and predicted climate change, while retaining the spirit of Johnston's garden.

Using drought-resistant varieties where appropriate reflects Johnston's interest in the Mediterranean and at the same time reduces the need for watering, while rainwater drawn from a spring on the hill rising to the east of the garden is used for irrigating garden areas that need it and for use in our visitor toilets. Water from the gardeners' wash-down pads is also recycled.

The garden is almost self-sufficient in compost production. All waste garden material is recycled through the compost heaps which are carefully attended to by the gardeners. Food waste from the catering outlets is recycled using a 'digester' which turns it into compost for the garden within weeks.

Growing forward

Hidcote is not only a masterpiece of garden design and planting, significantly it is also where the National Trust 'learnt to garden'. But like any learning, it is an ongoing process.

During the National Trust's custodianship, changing attitudes towards conservation, the availability of resources and the popularity of the garden have presented the Trust with many challenges, resulting in varying interpretations of Johnston's vision. However, the aim for horticultural excellence has remained constant. Now, with generous donations, recent research and a new approach to conservation, the garden is undergoing a gradual and sensitive programme to restore it as closely as possible to Johnston's original creation, selecting plants from the lists of those he is known to have kept and, with the use of historic photographs, returning the garden to its 1930s heyday.

Inevitably this has resulted in the need for more staff and the garden currently employs 12 gardeners working, together with a team of volunteers, to restore and maintain one of the country's most important gardens.

The practices learnt at Hidcote are being spread worldwide as gardeners from all corners of the globe are given an opportunity to work here. In exchange, Hidcote's gardeners have the chance to work abroad, sharing the knowledge they have acquired at Hidcote while learning new skills. This is very much in the spirit of Johnston's worldwide expeditions, reflected in the influences he brought back with him.

Hidcote is a reflection not only of the enormous contribution made to gardening by Lawrence Johnston, but also of the way the National Trust has learned by his example